Table of Cont

50 Hot Potato Questions for Christians

Matthew Robert Payne

Published by RWG Publishing, 2022.

50 Hot Potato Questions for Christians

Matthew Robert Payne

Dedication

I wish to dedicate this book to everyone who has unanswered questions, like me.

Introduction

The Christian life that I have lived has never been free of personal questions that I have had. As a teacher of the Word, I seem to have a never-ending list of questions about my faith. One day, some weeks ago, I sat down and wrote out on my computer a list of questions that the answers I have shared here may get me into hot water!

I hope that this moderate sized book sees you nodding your head in agreement more than you're turning your head in rejection of what has been said. Whatever the case, and whatever these hot potato questions spark in you, it is my prayer that this simple effort answers many of your long-held questions.

You could say that my answers about gay people and people living in sin are a little liberal in their leaning and more to the taste of hyper grace preachers, two positions that I don't hold most of the time. I look forward to your reviews on Amazon to let me know what you think.

Note on editing

These days I do not have the funds coming into my ministry to afford the most expensive editor money can buy. Please excuse me for any errors in this book that escaped our notice.

Question 1: Do you agree with gay marriage?

My personal belief is marriage is a union between men and women that was instituted in Genesis.

I believe that males are made for females and females are made for males, and the institution of marriage is between a male and a female. But after saying that, I understand that many gay and lesbian people don't understand the Bible, don't have a belief in the Bible, and aren't Christians. It's a Christian view that believes that marriage is between a male and a female. Because they don't necessarily believe in the Christian faith, they're not bound by the law of Christians; and the beliefs of Christians do not bind them. If the modern government wants to pass legislation that says two gay men can be married, the Christian church can't stand in their way. We have elected officials who are meant to uphold the law, write laws, and institute them.

We just so happened to have governments that legislated marriage, which can be between two gay men and two lesbians.

Personally, for myself, I say let them do what they want to do. Let them be responsible for their conscience and not have to conform to what I believe; after all, we are born into the world with free will. It was vital for God to allow his angels and human beings to have free will. Satan defected because angels were given free will and the same as a man's original sin, as they were told not to eat the fruit of the garden, but that's because God gave mankind free will. Because of that free will, gays can enter the institution of marriage, even though the Christian church doesn't believe in it.

I've had friends in the past in churches that were gay. I had someone I knew in a church who was a gay Christian, and he believed he could be gay. He thought he'd have to remain celibate to be on God's side. I was assured of his salvation, and that's what he believed. I interviewed

Freddie Mercury, the former lead singer of Queen, he was saved before he went to heaven, and he's in heaven. I've got a book called *Visiting Musicians in Heaven*. He's interviewed in that book. It will help if you're gay to read that interview and have some insight into the fact that Jesus has a lot of love in his heart for people with a gay inclination.

I don't mind gay people getting married. I don't believe marriage is an institution only for a male and a male. That's the answer to that question.

Question 2: Can a practicing gay person go to heaven?

I want to start this answer with the fact that I was addicted to pornography and prostitutes for over 40 years, and I lived in a cycle of addiction; I lived with falling for masturbating to porn, and then repenting and getting my peace back, and then falling again. I lived with regular attendance at the services of prostitutes. I'd repent, I'd say sorry for my sin, and I'd get my peace and my anointing back. Then shamefully, I'll do it again.

I believe that a person can be caught in a cycle of sin and honestly repent, say sorry to God, and be kept in a position of righteousness. Suppose a person is married to a gay person and living with a gay person and isn't feeling that they necessarily should repent of that situation. In that case, they're happy with it and not feeling remorse; I would leave it up to God whether God could see their hearts and forgive them.

I'm aware that many people will read this book and be outraged. It's like being asked by Oprah or a famous TV broadcaster. "What do I believe about gay couples? Would they go to heaven?" I will leave that in God's eyes. God is the one that weighs the heart.

I know there's a lot of Scripture in the Bible which would say a practicing gay person wouldn't go to heaven. Like I said, in answer to question one, I know that Freddie Mercury is in heaven. Jesus appeared to him in a vision as he died of cancer, and he gave his life to Jesus. He's interviewed in a book called "*Visiting Musicians in Heaven*," one of my books. Anything is possible with God.

I agree that many Scriptures in the Bible would say our practicing gay person isn't going to heaven. But I want to underline it with the fact that I was a practicing porn addict and addicted to prostitutes. Though I lived in guilt and condemnation and shame, for many years, in that lifestyle, I did sense the peace of God and their presence when I used to repent. Some lifestyles are hard to break, and some addictions are hard to break. I believe that I serve a God of mercy who's able to forgive, and he also knows the heart of a person and can judge the heart.

Do I believe a practicing gay person can go to heaven? I believe it's in God's hands. No one can understand what could happen right before that person dies. We can't envisage what God will do with the hearts of a person. So, it might not be the answer that you're looking for. But this is my personality. This is where I'm coming from.

Question 3: Can a Porn addict go to heaven?

As you've already read so far, in this book, I confessed that I had a 40-year addiction to pornography. I lived a life of falling into pornography, masturbation, and then repenting and getting my peace back.

Some would say I didn't properly repent because repenting stops the sin entirely. There's a lot of teaching in a church that would say, if I died in that state of participating in pornography and repenting, and then participating in it again, some would say, if I were in that cycle of addiction, of sin, to pornography, that I wouldn't go to heaven.

Some would say I'm willingly sinning, so I'm not repenting.

I've lived for many years under condemnation and guilt, and shame. I came to realize, finally, that Jesus loved me during my sin.

I received 50 or 100 personal prophecies in those years that said, Jesus is very happy with me, and Jesus is proud of me even during my sinful addictions; those prophecies won out. Some people listening to this would say that those prophecies were false and that I had false hope. Scripturally I was living a lifestyle of sin, and I couldn't possibly go to heaven.

I tend to think that when a person repents when a person prays to Jesus and says sorry for participating in sin, I believe that that person is forgiven, receives grace, and gets restored to a position of righteousness. I don't believe that many porn addicts, honestly doing it as a lifestyle, are unrepentant.

When they participate in sin, I feel that most porn addicts feel shameful and remorse, hopeless and unempowered, and weighed down by the sin, and shame and condemnation.

I don't believe many Christian men would live free of condemnation and guilt if they had a pornography addiction.

I believe that if I had died in that state of sin, if I was regularly practicing masturbating to pornography, I believe that my confession of my sin would have the grace of God, forgive me, and if I died, I would go to heaven. Do I believe that a person who masturbates to porn and then doesn't confess the sin that night, goes to sleep, and has a heart attack in a state of non-repentance goes to hell? Do I believe they go to heaven? I believe that Jesus knows the hearts of men, and Jesus and God weigh the hearts of men. If man was in a constant cycle of repenting for his sin, God and Jesus are aware of that, and that person would still get to heaven.

Of course, if Oprah, or a famous broadcaster, asked me this question, so many Christians would come out against me and label me a false teacher and a false prophet.

One of the reasons for doing this book is that it will give people a better picture of who I am as a Christian and as a Christian teacher.

Question 4: Can a person live in sin and go to heaven?

We're all sinners. Everyone who is a Christian is a sinner. I believe the Christians in the first century lived a lifestyle that was relatively free of sin. The apostle Paul and the apostle John lived relatively free of sin. I believe that is possible. Many Christians on this earth sin, and many commit habitual sin. Many Christians have their secret sins and are often confessing their sins.

We've already discussed that I believe someone addicted to porn, who continues to say sorry for his sin and restore his relationship with Jesus. I believe someone addicted to porn can be forgiven each time and go to heaven. They could even masturbate one night before going to bed and have a heart attack in their sleep without confessing their sin and still go to heaven.

I believe in a God full of mercy and have a good heart.

I believe a person could sin and still go to heaven.

The apostle John said in his letters, "He that sins have never known the Lord. He said that a believer comes away from sin, and the evil one doesn't touch him."

We've got Scripture that says, "It's possible not to sin." But I know from my track record that I had sinned. For many years, I was in addiction to pornography and prostitutes, and I can't say that those sins are over, even though I've had a reprieve.

I understood that certain people wouldn't go to heaven. I understand that certain Christians won't go to heaven. I believe that someone caught in a sin cycle, continually cycling back to a sinful lifestyle, can be forgiven each time they repent. If they're living in a sin that you're not repented of, if they're living with someone else's wife in a state of adultery, or if you're living with a partner, then they may not be forgiven. If you are not married but living in a constant state of fornication; if you're living a lifestyle of sin and not repenting, each time for the sin, but blatantly living in sin, I don't believe that you would get heaven. I believe that God is the judge.

I believe if you're in a state of repeated sin you're not repenting; for instance, you're living with another man's wife or in a relationship outside of marriage you are in trouble. You're in continual fornication- or you're gay, and you're married and living in a constant state of fornication, as single males and females live together in fornication- there's a chance that even if you're saved and Christian, you won't go to heaven.

I can't give a definitive answer. I know that God and Jesus have been merciful in my case, and sometimes I wonder whether you could commit a sin so many times and be forgiven. I wondered if there was a limit to Jesus' forgiveness, but I've committed sins, and sexual immorality, so many times, and I was forgiven so many times that I think God continues to forgive.

I hope this answer has blessed you.

Question 5: Can you teach wrong theology and not be a false teacher?

I wouldn't say I like the term false teacher and a false prophet. I have an aversion to it. I am not sure I would label anyone a false prophet or teacher, even though they're mentioned in the Bible. You can have an understanding that people will be taken in a rapture midway through the tribulation, and you could be wrong about that. The right theology may be a pretribulation rapture. I don't consider you a false teacher if you're teaching that currently. I believe there'll be a pretribulation rapture, a rapture midway through the tribulation and a rapture at the end. So, I believe in a three-rapture theory.

Should I be considered a false teacher for believing that? Some people teach legalistic doctrine about an angry God, full of rules and a God of wrath, and a God of judgment. They teach a doctrine of legalism, and they wouldn't like this book, and they wouldn't like my answers that are given in this book.

Should they be called a false teacher if they're teaching this rigid, angry God doctrine? Because much of my Christian experience was under their indoctrination. They used many Scripture verses to support their way of thinking and their theology. If what they're teaching is a wrong and incorrect doctrine, should they be called false teachers? I don't believe they should be.

I'm very innocent and pure. I've got an innocent, childlike faith. I have a hard time believing that a person would purposely teach error. If someone knew what they were teaching was an error, they were doing it to earn money or remain popular, that is a worry. Still, they knew what they were teaching was an error, and now were doing it on purpose; I believe that person would be able to be classified as a false teacher.

For instance, some people who teach the prosperity doctrine know that the teaching is false. I would consider them false teachers, but most pastors and people teaching the Word of God are trying to do it with some form of sincerity and honesty. If they're honestly wrong with their theology, if they're honestly teaching something that is in error, I don't personally believe they're a false teacher. I'd only consider a false teacher who's teaching error and doing it on purpose for more popularity, finances, and power.

There certainly would be people who do that. But because of my innocent nature, I believe in the good of humanity; I believe in the good of teachers. I would find it very hard. I'd find it very hard to teach something I knew was wrong; I wouldn't be able to do it.

Consider this book; it's got some controversial questions in it. But I don't believe that I would rightly be called a false teacher or a false prophet by people who will write reviews for this on Amazon.

I know false teachers and prophets are mentioned in prophecy and the Bible. And Paul mentions in Timothy that "People raise teachers that will tickle itching ears." Some false teachers exist, although I don't believe many people do it on purpose.

I hope you learned something from this teaching.

Question 6: What is a false prophet?

What is a false prophet? Many believe a person is a false prophet if they teach false doctrine or theology. We just covered that you can be teaching false theology or wrong theology and not be called a false teacher. I would consider that most people have beliefs and doctrines that they believe in that are false. I believe that many teachers of the Word of God have false theology and doctrines in the number of things they believe.

There's a Scripture in the Old Testament that says something like a prophet shouldn't be respected or honored as a prophet if their prophecies don't come true. Some people will consider a person a false prophet if they prophesy something and it doesn't come true. We saw lately, in the last couple of years, many prophets prophesied that Trump would have a second term, and he didn't. There are many videos by people calling those prophets that got it wrong, false prophets.

I don't believe a prophet who gets a prophecy wrong should be labeled false. They should not be called false prophets if they got a corporate or personal prophecy wrong. That's a personal belief, a personal understanding that prophets in the New Testament can miss and get a prophecy wrong. In the Old Testament, the people of God didn't have the Holy Spirit to discern whether a prophecy was right or wrong. It was more important in the prophets being accurate.

I would consider a false prophet, what the Old Testament says, a Prophet that leads you to serve other gods. The other god could be money and the world. Someone is teaching the prosperity message; the prosperity gospel teaches you to serve the world, serve money, and make money as your God. They would be leading you into error. They would lead you to serve a false God, Mammon. A Prophet who is teaching people to serve, idolize, and build them up as a pseudo-God could also be considered a false prophet.

I remember having a friend who would talk for hours about a supposed prophet's teachings and stories, and she would talk for hours about what this person had said.

I asked her once, "Could you speak for an hour about what Jesus taught?"

She said, "No."

I said, "But you can speak for hours about what this other person has said; this other person has become a false prophet in your eyes and has become an idol."

A false prophet could teach you to serve another god or serve them.

That's my definition of a false prophet. I don't know of any false prophets; besides that person; I was talking about referencing there. I'm unaware of many false prophets, but if someone's teaching the prosperity doctrine, you could call them false.

I pray that you are encouraged by the answer to this question.

Question 7: Should you call out ministries in error?

Should you call ministries out in error and be a person who has spoken against the anointed? I used to be a person who called ministries out that I believed were in error. I believe that this was an error on my part.

I feel that the best way to go about calling someone out in error isn't to make a YouTube video about the ministry and the error but to post it on Facebook the error or get a video where someone else's done that in a public forum on a YouTube video, and post what the other person has said. I don't believe that we should be pulling each other down.

You may wonder, well, how are people going to find out about how this person is in error? I would leave that to the Holy Spirit to help people discern it.

I propose you go to the ministry's website and get your contact and email address. You send your letter there privately, informing the ministry of your concerns or bringing corrections to the ministry.

Please understand that when you need to correct a ministry, you move in pride and self-righteousness. That's the case; you are often filled with pride and self-righteousness, thinking you're better than the ministry. I've just found that to be the case in my life. I encourage you to write to the ministry. But first, before you do anything, I would encourage you to take the matter to prayer and pray until you're in a position of humility and write the letter with respect and humility. As you present your argument, I'm sure you may include Scriptures to back up and support what you're saying.

Remember, the Scriptures are in the Bible to edify and exalt us. They're not in the Bible to be used in rebukes and corrections. The letter to Timothy said it could be used like that. But, if you're using the Scriptures in the Bible as a sword, the Scriptures in the Bible are meant to be used as a sword against Satan, not against other ministers in the ministry.

I encourage you to write a private letter to a minister and bathe the whole situation in prayer to come to the minister in the spirit of humility. That's what I have to say on the subject.

I hope you're encouraged by this chapter.

Question 8: What is your view on the rapture?

For over twenty years, I believed in a post-tribulation rapture. I believed that the two witnesses would come at the beginning of the tribulation, and they would minister for three and a half years and be killed, lie on the street for three days, and then rise from the dead. I believed when they rose from the dead and went into the air, that would be the time of the rapture.

For twenty years or so, I was angry with people who believed in a pretribulation rapture. I would get angry with people who espoused that view of the pretribulation rapture. I felt that people didn't deserve to go into a pretribulation rapture. I was adamant that most people would go halfway through the Tribulation.

As part of a Zoom meeting once a week, which I'm still part of, the leader of that Zoom group taught on the pretribulation rapture. He's very knowledgeable in things of God. One week, he shared that he believed in the pretribulation rapture, and God used that as he anointed that word. God had a breakthrough with me. Reading a book based on the pretribulation rapture, God convinced me that the pretribulation rapture was true.

Eric, who teaches the Zoom group, believed there was a pretribulation rapture, but the only people that were going to leave Earth on the pretribulation rapture were the Bride of Christ. The Bride of Christ is a certain percentage of Christians whose lives are set apart for God and holy. It's only a small percentage of Christians, and that understanding struck me that the average pew sitter who sits on pews and doesn't do anything in the Christian church would miss the rapture. It was a way of me having my cake and eating it too.

I believe that the average Christian if they're not passionate about Jesus and heaven, become intimate with Jesus, haven't gotten a life of intimacy with Jesus, will miss out on the pretribulation rapture and must wait until halfway through the tribulation when the two witnesses die.

I came to understand that as my view on the rapture. I further understood that there would be three raptures, the pretribulation rapture and the rapture midway through the tribulation. Then there'll be people that will be taken off the Earth at the end of the tribulation, meet Jesus in the air, and then come back to Earth and reign with Christ. I believe in three separate raptures.

You don't have to accept what I believe in you. This is one of the doctrines, one of the understandings that someone can have that isn't essential for salvation. But I would encourage you to get an intimate relationship with Jesus and become the Bride of Christ, or I believe you'll miss out on the first rapture.

I hope this has encouraged you and given you some clarity about where and what I believe.

Question 9: Is the rapture imminent?

I believe many things must happen before the rapture; there must be a worldwide revival before Jesus returns.

I tend to sense that Jesus and God His Father aren't happy with the number of Christians worldwide.

I believe there must be more Christians before we see a rapture. Things must form for the establishment of the Antichrist. We've seen the One World Government moving towards that now. But I think it's too early, and their plans are going to be postponed by God. An Antichrist can't come in without God's permission. I don't believe that Jesus is coming back anytime soon.

I live a life consecrated to the Lord, and I'm very close to the Lord, and I'm the Bride of Christ and have an intimate relationship with Jesus, and I'm ready to go at any time. I believe that the prophecy of Isaiah 60 must be manifested in the world. Christians must shine brightly with the manifest presence of Jesus, and the world needs to become darker before the return of Jesus.

Many people who teach on YouTube believe the rapture will happen at any moment. I don't believe that personally is true. I don't even believe there will be a rapture in my lifetime; I believe I'll die a natural death or death due to some disease before the rapture occurs. I don't believe Jesus will return in the next 20 or 30 years.

These questions address things I believe, and many people would take issue with my answer here.

I know of an Indian apostle who has planted 600 churches and promised the Lord that he would plant 1500 churches. The Lord Jesus visits him every year on his birthday in the flesh. He's got a good relationship with Jesus. I believe he will fulfill his promise, and he has been going for 20 years with 600 churches. I believe that he'll continue and plant 1500 churches.

That's what I believe.

Question 10: Can we live a sinless life?

In my life, I have met two apostles; they were people who claimed to be apostles. Both their Bibles had many similarities. They were filled with notes and annotations in the margins and notes in the text that was heavily highlighted.

Both men, I asked the question, "Do you ever sin?" One of them lived in my apartment for six weeks. In the fifth week, I asked him, "Do you ever sin?"

He said, "No."

I said, "Where is it said in the Bible that's possible?"

He said, "Romans 6 and other places".

He said, at the time, he didn't have time to show me the Bible, but he'll make time. The next day, he sat me down and walked me through the Bible and how many Bible references proved that you didn't have to sin. I've since come to realize that you can live a sinless life, you can live a life where you've sinned in the past, but you no longer sin. I haven't attained that lifestyle myself yet.

I wasn't there when he was asked, but the other apostle was asked, "Do you ever sin?" He said, "Not very often, and when I do, they are small ones."

1 John 2:6 says, "He abides in Him must walk just as He walked." If you take that Scripture literally, that means that if you've got a close and intimate relationship with Jesus and say that you do, you should behave like Jesus. We know that Jesus didn't sin.

The apostle Paul, in Corinthians, said, "Imitate me as I imitate the Lord." Once again, if the Apostle Paul imitated the Lord, he wouldn't be sinning. He told folks in the Corinthian church to imitate him, which points to a holy life.

John, in his letters, says, "Anyone who knows the Lord does not sin, and the evil one has no part of him." John wouldn't write those things in his epistles if he were still sinning and couldn't walk sin-free.

It may be something that's far off for you. It may be something that seems impossible for you. The Lord has mercy, forgiveness, and grace toward us. I certainly need the grace of the Lord in my life, but it is possible. If you're living alive, relatively sin-free yourself. It is possible.

I hope this chapter will encourage you to live a sinless life. I hope that you got something from this. I have certainly met two men that were sin-free.

Question 11: What is Holiness?

I believe holiness is more than just a state of righteousness; holiness also has to do with largely if we've been set apart from the world. James makes it clear in James 4:4 that "When you're a friend of the world, you become an enemy of God." I tend to think that if you're an enemy of God, you're not going to make it into Heaven.

Jesus was clear in the book of Revelation, where he says, "The people were never hot nor cold, but were lukewarm because of the riches." They felt that they did not need God. It was an accumulation of riches that the people had that was affecting their walk. Jesus called them lukewarm and said he would "vomit them out of his mouth." One thing I know about vomit is when you vomit; something is very unpleasant. You don't pick up the vomit and put it back into your mouth, saying, "This is my body; I'm going to collect it and put it back where it came from." If Jesus vomited part of his body out, it's part that will not come back.

I believe a holy person, per see, is someone who truly pleases God. They have a life that focuses on God and solely on God; they have certain interests that please God. They have a way about them that pleases God. They're not entangled with the things of the world.

Jesus said, in the parable of the soils, that "People didn't bear fruit because we are entangled with the riches of the world and the lust for the things of the world."

In the parable of the soils, he showed that fruit could stop being present in a person's life. Jesus wants you to focus on him and his Kingdom. He wants you to delight in him and his Kingdom, and he doesn't want you to focus your attention or your resources on the things of the world. He wants you to focus solely on him, his way of life, and his Kingdom for you to be holy.

Peter encourages us to be holy, just as God is holy. We've got the command to do that.

It takes a process to come out of the world and to leave the world behind; it involves leaving possessions. It's a leaving of spending habits; it's leaving certain friends and acquaintances. It's a process that is needed. I encourage you to follow that process. God bless you, and I hope that you learned something.

Question 12: Is it possible to see God's face and live?

Scripture makes the case that it isn't possible to see God's face and live. I feel that we misunderstand that Scripture.

On a visit to Heaven, I saw God on His throne as a ball of light. I remember working with a counselor who said, "Jesus is a ball of light." The counselor said, "You should be able to see his face. It's a religious spirit stopping you from seeing his face." I took that on board with some spiritual entity. Soon enough, after healing, I could see his face."

I know there's Scripture that says you can't see God's face and live. But my testimony is that I've seen God's face. I had a series called, Conversations with God. I had four books. In the third book, Conversations with God Book 3, I saw God's face. I was writing the conversations on my computer, and God was visiting me from Heaven in my house. He would sit on the sofa and talk to me face to face, and several times, he got emotional and cried.

I remember seeing God's face because I could see the tears running down his cheeks when he cried. I'm a person who is either deceived or deceived in my visions of a person who has seen God's face and lived to tell the story. I prefer to think I'm someone who saw God's face and lived to tell the story. I'm quite open to being deceived. I've been deceived many times in the past. I still have a good, vibrant relationship with the Lord. I still have an intimate relationship with the Lord, no matter how often I have been deceived.

I've come to understand that I have been deceived about certain things. But in this instance, I don't believe that I was deceived. I sensed that I was looking upon the face of God and seeing his tears for what they were.

He said to me, at one stage, he couldn't express the love that he had for me in English words. And so, he was crying to express his love for

27

me. I have experienced the vision of God where I saw his face. You also can experience God's face and experience God for yourself. I encourage you to seek God in Heaven and seek God in your relationship, and don't be afraid to approach him, and don't be afraid and held back by the theology that says that you can't see him.

Question 13: Is it possible to visit Heaven without dying?

I know, personally myself, the answer is yes. I have had visions in my mind several times and visited Heaven. The first time I had a vision of Heaven, I was led by a counselor. The counselor was talking to me and said that I was going to see something in my imagination. He told me to tell him what it was. I said, "I'm in Heaven and can see Jesus." He counseled me through a vision, and I had an encounter with Jesus. He took me into the throne room, and I met God, conversed with God, and met many saints from Heaven, who came and stood before me and paid their respects to me.

It is possible to visit Heaven without dying. You'll find that there are several books on the subject written by people who've been to Heaven, and they can be quite enjoyable to read, and I have been used several times to help people see Heaven. I have a special place in Heaven, a "portal in Heaven" where I can take people in their imagination to see and enter Heaven through this portal set up for me.

The first time I took a person to Heaven was by faith. I held his hand and described something for him to imagine. When he imagined what I was describing, he experienced Heaven and could see Heaven.

On my website, I have a service where I can; for a donation, I can take people to Heaven. I don't offer that service to make money, although the money does help to finance my books; I do it so that people can experience Heaven for themselves.

It can be hard on you when you go to Heaven. Heaven is full of the glory of the Lord and a strong presence of the Lord.

Because of that strong presence of the Lord, it makes you feel good. Feeling good can shock your system to return to Earth and have the glory leave you. So, visiting Heaven isn't one of my favorite occupations because I wouldn't say I like experiencing the glory and then having the glory depart from my life.

I have visited Heaven many times, and I've got a book called, *My Visits to Heaven, Lessons Learned*. That book shows several visits to Heaven that I've had.

Question 14: Do the sizes of people's mansions in Heaven vary?

I've done a series of books, visiting saints in Heaven and saints' mansions in Heaven. The mansions all seemed quite large. They were all saints of the Bible and saints that had a good reputation since Christ. But we're reminded in Scripture that we will all be rewarded according to our works on Earth.

I have heard the Holy Spirit say that people's mansions vary in size according to their works and what they did on Earth. The simple answer is that the size of your mansion will be different from the size of someone else's mansion, according to the work you did with your life.

God makes it very clear in the Word of God that works are important. The fact is that we will be rewarded in Heaven according to our works. I don't think you can expect if you go to church, sit in a pew, and attend church each week, and live a life without reaching people, without touching people, without influencing people for the Gospel, without tithing, without giving to the Lord, doing nothing towards the Kingdom essentially, and then be rewarded with great rewards in Heaven.

You won't be rewarded as much as someone who gave their whole life to Jesus and gave their whole life to the Kingdom of God.

Everyone that goes to Heaven will be happy with their experience of Heaven. I sense that people will enjoy Heaven when they get to Heaven. But I am persuaded by what the Scriptures say that the reward level in Heaven will vary according to what people have done on earth with their life.

If you are reading this, I encourage you to find your purpose. Find out how to live your purpose and how you can invest your life in doing Kingdom works for Jesus and prospering with the Kingdom with your life. I encourage you to live a life of good works rather than just sitting around doing nothing for the Kingdom. I pray that this will encourage you.

Question 15: How does God judge people that never heard the Gospel?

One understanding I have about God is that God is a God of second chances and mercy. People who are in a village in India, who've never heard of Jesus, who's never heard of the Gospel, what happens to those people? I believe that people that have never heard the Gospel of Jesus in Jesus' name get judged by the parable of the sheep and the goats, which says I was hungry, I was thirsty, I was naked and poor, I was in prison, and you visited me, and you gave me something to drink and eat. I sense that people are judged by their hearts, by what sort of heart they have.

I believe God judges people, accordingly, depending on what sort of person they are. Of course, many people would bring up the verse in John 14:6 "I'm the way, the truth, and the life; no man goes to the Father except through me." They will take exception to what I'm saying here.

This has always been a question on my mind; if you think about it, it is on many people's minds. I remember one time I got angry with God. I was cussing at him and saying if the Christians are true, and people in India that I met in villages that don't know Jesus, if they die, and don't go to Heaven, I don't want to go to Heaven either. I don't want to be part of a God like that. I said that my uncle and auntie, good people, must go to hell. I don't want to be part of a system like that.

God listened to my tirade. Then, at the end of it, he laughed. He asked me if I was finished. He said that he's not like the Christians make him out to be and that there's plenty of mercy in his kingdom. He reassured me that things aren't as bad as Christians make them out to be.

That's my answer to the question, I believe. The people who have never heard of Jesus are judged by the sheep and the goat's parable.

Even Christians are judged by the sheep and the goat's parable. If they don't measure up to the sheep and the goat's parable, they won't end up in Heaven. I believe everyone on Earth who finds themselves in Heaven will have a lifestyle meeting the demands of the sheep and goat's parable. Perhaps you might want to go and read it for yourself and see if your life is lining up. I pray that this chapter helps you.

Question 16: What happens to people who never understood the Gospel?

It seems unfair for someone who never understood the Gospel message when it was explained to them to go to hell. It seems quite unfair that that person would go to hell for that. Isn't it more up to the side of the person explaining the Gospel? Isn't it their duty to explain the Gospel properly? Surely, a person who has heard the Gospel and didn't quite understand what it meant to be free of guilt? Surely, they wouldn't be judged?

In answer to this question, I would side with the mercy of God. Once again, as in the previous question, I asked what happens to people who've never heard the Gospel. My answer was that those people are judged, I believe, by the merits of the sheep and the goat's parable. If they had a good heart and were good to people, according to the righteousness of the sheep and the goat's parable, I believe they'd go to Heaven. I believe the same is true of people who don't understand the Gospel; I would say that they would be judged by the merits of the sheep and the goat's parable.

I lived a life of a lot of sin; I had sexual addictions. I lived many years of my life in sin. I've had six months outside of the sin where I've conquered it, fallen again to temptation, and fallen back into it. I know God as a God of mercy. I know God as a forgiving God. I tend to have a good relationship with God and understand him quite well. I can't see a person who, for no fault of their own, can't understand the Gospel and doesn't fully understand the Gospel message being judged for it. They aren't rejecting the Gospel when they don't accept Jesus as a Savior because they don't understand it. Because of that lack of understanding, I can't see them judged and sent to hell.

I would side with the mercy of God. I'd side with God's mercy in this situation. I believe God would make way for them to come into the Kingdom. There are a lot of good-hearted people in the world, a lot of genuine, beautiful people that live in our society and never really understand the Gospel message and haven't gotten the ability to respond to the Gospel message simply because they don't understand it. I would side with the mercy of God in this situation. I pray that you've been blessed by this message and saw something you understood.

Question 17 Does reward in Heaven vary?

We are told in Scripture that God will reward everyone according to their deeds. When you give a homeless person Coca-Cola, or you give a homeless person $2, you can bet there will be a reward in Heaven for it. I have lived a life that is often focused on reward; I have lived a life of love and have been led to be generous to the poor.

First, because of love, I empathize with the homeless and understand them because I used to be homeless. First, I give to them because of my love, empathy, and compassion. But secondly, I give to the poor because I know there will be rewards in Heaven.

I self-publish books because I love to write, and I love to educate, and I love to teach. That's the first motivation because I love to teach and affect people's lives. I also love hearing the feedback and reviews people write on my books. So that's a second motivation. But thirdly, I like the idea that I'll get rewarded in Heaven, not only for producing the books but also get a reward for the finances spent in making the books happen.

I believe there will be a reward in Heaven, which will vary according to what people do.

You'll remember, in the parable of the talents and the minas, the master gave the servants a certain amount of money for the talents. He gave one five talents, one two talents, and another one talent. He gave them money according to their abilities. Then he came back, and the one with five talents had returned five. He said that he would reward him with having control over several cities. He delegated the reward according to what he did.

So, we've had for our scriptural basis for the same variance in rewards. Rewards will vary in Heaven, and it's up to you to do the work on Earth and do things worthy of reward. On Earth, you've only got one opportunity to store eternal rewards for yourself. Therefore, get to it, and do things you know the Lord would be happy with. I pray that this has blessed you.

Question 18: Are there different realms in Heaven?

I have read certain books by certain authors. I think Sadhu Sundar Singh had a book about realms in Heaven and the fact that the different realms in Heaven are tied to Heavenly rewards; the more you do on Earth, the greater realm you will exist in, in Heaven.

According to these writers, you can't go to Heaven and meet the patriarchs of the faith; it's up to them, as led by the Holy Spirit, to come down from their realm to visit you.

So, patriarchs and people from a higher realm could be walking through the main city of Heaven and only meeting people in their realm. You could walk past them and not even know they are there.

The idea of rewards in Heaven is abhorrent to some people. Some people consider the concept of rewards in Heaven to be a disgraceful subject to be subject that they don't want to think about. Some people consider that you should be able to live a normal Christian life without doing anything for the Lord, participating in winning souls or financing ministries that save souls, and essentially doing nothing to save other people. They expect to be rewarded like everyone else in Heaven.

Some people consider living this normal, uneventful life on earth and consider that they should have the same reward as everyone else. We know that that doesn't happen on earth. We know that winning the lottery is one of the only ways of becoming wealthy without doing anything. We know that if you work hard and are diligent, you can make money, but no one resting on their laurels can make money and become successful and rich. So too, it is in Heaven that people who have contributed in a major way on earth to the Kingdom's purposes. make themselves a path and create a realm where they will survive in Heaven.

By knowing that there are different realms in Heaven and levels of enjoyment, I strive to do everything possible with my talents and life. I dedicate my time, resources, intellect, and faith to doing things that will reward me greatly in Heaven.

As a reader of this book, I encourage you to find out what you're destined to do. Find out your purpose and do your purpose with vigor. Participate in your purpose with everything that's within you because the reward in Heaven will vary according to your work on earth. I pray that this will stir you into action!

Question 19: Does the Holy Spirit lead you into truth and out of error?

Does the Holy Spirit lead you into Truth and out of error? The Holy Spirit in the Scriptures is called the Spirit of Truth.

Jesus told his disciples that the Holy Spirit would come after him and lead them into all Truth. The Holy Spirit is a force in your life, the personal aspect of God that is used to lead you into Truth. You can be a person who is in error, who believes certain doctrines and theologies that can be in error, and the Holy Spirit has the power and the ability to lead you into Truth and lead you away from the error that you find yourself in.

At one stage, I was in a delusion that lasted for 16 years. I believe I was one of two witnesses mentioned in Revelation chapter 11. I firmly believed that for 16 years, no one could talk me out of it. Then one day, a young prophet or a young person, new to the prophetic gift, came to me and said Jesus had said something on the train to 'him' on the way out to my place. He said I wouldn't be happy with what 'Jesus' said. Jesus told him to tell me something. He made me promise that I wasn't going to get angry. I promised him I wouldn't get angry. Then he told me that I wasn't one of the two witnesses. Although I'd been in delusion for 16 years, the power of the Holy Spirit was in his words, bringing me out of that delusion. I didn't believe that delusion of mine anymore. The Holy Spirit, in his words, the presence of God, pulled me out of that delusion.

I believed, for many years, like I've shared, that we will have a rapture midway through the Tribulation. I didn't believe in a pretribulation rapture. I now believe in the pretribulation rapture, and God used the Holy Spirit to minister to me and directed me to that belief. So, the Holy Spirit is powerful and can lead you into Truth.

The Holy Spirit can bring sermons that you heard and certain Truths that you heard in the past that you may not have been aware of at the time; he's able to bring the Truth to your remembrance. The Holy Spirit ministered to the disciples who wrote the Gospels.

They could remember the words of Jesus and the things that Jesus did in consecutive order by the power of the Holy Spirit and the ability of the Holy Spirit. The Holy Spirit is powerful and can lead us into Truth and out of error.

Question 20: Will Joel Osteen and what others call false teachers go to Heaven?

I used to be a person who was critical of other ministries. I used to call ministries out and call teachers out and call them false prophets and false teachers. Instead of calling them out, the Holy Spirit led me to pray for them, have a spirit of humility about me, and come away from the prideful way of self-righteousness and thinking too highly of myself.

I have to say, in my years of addictions and sexual sin, being a person who sinned a lot over the last 40 years, it becomes tiresome to hear people post messages about people who, according to sin, are going to hell. The Christian church isn't very graceful, caring, and compassionate to people caught in addiction. They have a very hard line when it comes to sin and is very abrupt with people in how they share and post information.

In that climate, people like Joel Osteen do the world a good service, preaching happy, encouraging, and uplifting messages. The people of God are often beaten down and overcome with life's struggles and trials. I can see a real need for them to be encouraged, built up, and blessed by someone like Joel.

I've only heard one of his sermons, although his wife is a friend on Facebook. I follow her page, and she has many encouraging things to say. I'm always reading what she has to say.

I'm cautious and hesitant to call someone a false prophet or false teacher, as I shared earlier when discussing a false prophet. I believe a false prophet leads you to serve another God, whether money or themselves, and I can't see Joel Osteen causing people to serve him. I can't see him leading people to serve another God. I don't believe that Joel is a false teacher. The many people who act like the police for the Christian church, who some call heresy hunters, would disagree with this assessment, and they often name Joel Osteen in a list of false teachers.

I tend to be used to the grace of God and the mercy of God being applied to me, with myself being forgiven multiple times by God. It's put me in a position and a state of mind that allows me to extend mercy and grace. I tend to have changed my attitude regarding preachers and teachers in the body of Christ, and I apply a lot of grace to them.

I believe God will judge you if you're a false teacher and teaching error on purpose. I pray that you've been encouraged by this.

Question 21: Am I more worried about my judgment as a teacher?

That Scripture verse that says, "You come under stricter judgment as a teacher," has never personally worried me. I'm aware that as a teacher, I need to be right about what I teach. I know I could be wrong in my beliefs and doctrine about certain things. Of course, I care about teaching errors. I'm just not too concerned about it. If you had to wait until all you taught was correct doctrine, you would never start to teach!

I've got a right heart. I've got the right motive. I live to inform, encourage, and build people up with what I teach. I do my best to stay out of error. I do my best to discover the Truth on matters. I read a lot, and I study a lot. I do my best to stay informed about certain subjects.

One subject that I have read a lot on is the study of Revelation and end times. There are various views and understandings about the book of Revelation. It cannot be very clear. There are so many Scripture verses that support multiple raptures. I'm aware of that. I'm aware of different Biblical teachers' different points of view. They can't all be right. Yet, people teach with such authority that you pay attention to what they say and as they use Biblical references to support what they say.

I like to support what I say with Scripture when I can. It's just that I have not been able to read the Bible for years. I lack Biblical verses to quote to support my views.

You'll find very few Biblical references in this book, largely because I stopped reading the New Testament since I was burned out by teachers of the Word of God who used Scriptures to support what they had to say.

First, Legalism took me and deceived me. Then the grace movement took me and deceived me. I tended to see that both points of view were supported by teachers using the Scriptures. I tended to hold the Bible accountable for leading me astray. I stopped reading the Bible because the verses in the Bible reminded me of the false teaching.

I teach, and I share, and I like to try and support myself with Scripture when I can. I'm not afraid of stricter judgment because I'm doing things from a good place in my heart. I hope this encouraged you and you saw some insight into where I'm coming from.

Question 22: Why does Jesus allow so much error in the church?

I asked my friend Dundy about this question. He said he "allows an error in the church so that people may learn." We tend to only learn from our mistakes, and we learn from errors.

I mentioned that for 16 years, I believed I was one of two witnesses of Revelation, chapter 11. For 16 years, I was in a delusion, which is a long time to be in a delusion. In that delusional state, I read the Old Testament prophets and the book of Revelation many times. I learned a lot, and I gleaned a lot from Scripture. It was a learning experience for me.

You wouldn't be able to say that I was stagnant in my faith. My faith was invigorated. I was able to prophesy over people correctly. I flowed in the gifts of the Holy Spirit. But I was in error. I made a personal error. I believed I was an end times prophet, which wasn't true!

I learned a tremendous amount. When there's an error in the church, there's room for people who are in that error to learn. The people of God are meant to be encouraged to correct each other, come alongside, and bring each other out of error. The error allows the body of Christ to function. Well, it allows the body of Christ to work in a conducive way toward each other.

Error isn't a good thing. A person who's in error isn't necessarily helpful. For his reasons, Jesus tends to allow error in the church.

Perhaps you're a person who believes that you don't believe any error. Perhaps you're a person who is confident that everything that you believe, doctrinally, is the truth. I take my hat off to you if that's what you believe.

I believe everyone in the world is in some form of error or believes in some form of error. If you're free of error, that's almost like saying you're free of sin. I've discussed that I've met people free of sin before, which is possible, but I believe Jesus allows an error in a church for the church to experience growth.

Question 23: Why is there suffering?

I'm a person who has bipolar disorder and schizophrenia and suffers most days. Most days, my sleeping is affected. Bipolar affects your life. It's difficult to be seen as someone who's mentally ill and not always in the right mind, so I understand the position of suffering.

Why does God allow it? I feel that suffering and sickness come from the sin of Adam and Eve. I believe suffering came into the world as soon as man sinned. I feel that sickness and suffering are a consequence of sin. It's just something that we must put up with in the world.

Jesus can provide solace for people who suffer. Jesus can draw close to you when you're a person who suffers. You can develop a close relationship with Jesus as you suffer. In a sense, there's a lot of suffering in the world because man has free will and does some despicable things. God has allowed humanity to have free will, choices, and the ability to choose. Some men are evil, and they choose evil.

Some men put women, children, and men in situations where they are trafficked as enslaved people, and there's tremendous suffering for all involved. It is horrific that God would allow that. Although if he didn't allow that, we'd have a God constantly interrupting humanity and coming to the rescue of humanity, and we wouldn't live our lives as free individuals. We wouldn't exercise a life of free will.

Some said God didn't want to create robots and didn't want people to do what he wanted automatically. Therefore, one of the outcomes of allowing a man to have free will is the potential for men to do damage and cause people to suffer.

I know any specific person didn't cause my mental illness. I know my mental illness was genetic. I did have a hard situation of a custody fight that helped me have my first breakdown. A situation caused it with my former wife. But I coped, and I've developed a good relationship with Jesus. Suffering draws you close to Jesus. I feel compassion and empathy for people who suffer. Suffering isn't a good thing. It's one of those questions that remains a mystery to some.

I hope that I've helped you understand a little bit about suffering. I hope to mention that I suffered helped. I pray that this chapter has helped.

Question 24: Is God really in control?

It says in Scripture that Satan has become the god of this world. Satan has his way often in the world.

To say that God is in control can cause a lot of pain in victims. One example I heard a Bible teacher share where a young boy was killed when a drunk driver crashed his motor vehicle into his, and the boy was being laid to rest. The pastor, in that instance, said that God was in control and this accident happened in his will. Can you imagine how the people thought about the God who allowed that death?

Many bad things happen in the world that God is not in control of because he has given humanity free will. He's given men the ability to choose, which all started in Eden's garden. Humanity has been making bad choices ever since then!

All the abuse that happens in this world, all the slave trafficking and sexual abuse and rape and murder that happens in this world, isn't controlled by God. God does not control the evil things that humanity does. It can be a misconception of some believers, some Christians who believe God is in control.

God is sovereign, and his understanding of things is full of wisdom, mercy, and grace. He's got some wonderful attributes, but he's not in control of what goes on down here. Humanity upsets him and disappoints him.

If God were in control, even of the Christian church, Christians would obey his Son. Jesus had 50 commandments. He had 50 things that he told his followers to do. Not more than 2% of Christians are aware that Jesus has 50 commandments and therefore obey what he taught them to do. Jesus taught a narrow way. It is a difficult way of obedience that is hard to adhere to. The Christian church doesn't obey him most of the time. The world would be better if the church's Christians obeyed him, but they don't! God isn't even in control of his church. The people who are meant to be pleasing him, those who are meant to be following him, don't understand him or understand what he requires of them.

If the Christian church isn't obedient if the followers of God don't follow God, what state does that leave the rest of the world in? God is not in control. He's not even in control of his church. It can hurt people suffering already in this life, through debilitating illness or hardship, to say that God is in control. When people suffer hardship and suffering in their bodies, the worst thing they can think of is that God organized that pain; when you are deceived into thinking that God is in control and you share that with a person suffering pain, it breaks them further than the pain.

God is not in control. He has desires and wants that he wants humanity to achieve. He is a gentleman, he doesn't insist on his way, and he allows humanity to have free will and to determine what they do with their lives in different situations. I pray that this has informed you and encouraged you.

Question 25: Is the church asleep and lukewarm?

I believe that large amounts of the church are lukewarm and asleep.

Jesus shared with the church of Laodicea in the book of Revelation that they were neither hot nor cold but lukewarm because they depended on their riches. They believed that they were rich and needed nothing. That's largely the state of the Western Church. Many people in the church don't need God. They only seem to pray to God for their selfish needs and desires. But their day-to-day life can be lived without God, without the presence of God.

So many Christians are unaware of the presence of God and don't walk in a day-by-day relationship with God and obedience.

The church is often filled with lukewarm people with no zeal and fire for the Holy Spirit. They have people who go through the motions of religion but aren't revivalists and people who wake up society and influence society. They're not world changers. They're not people who can change the circumstances of unbelievers and can influence them. Many people in the church are simply asleep, of course, doing religious things. They attend church, sing, praise, and worship songs to feel the presence of God. They listen to sermons, read their Bible, and do holy things, but they're asleep. They have no idea of the season we're in; they have no idea of the thoughts of God and the inner workings of God's Kingdom. They are fast asleep.

I thought the Coronavirus and the problem we had with that would wake them up. With all its issues and concerns, I thought the pandemic would wake the church, but it seemed to have failed. The churches are sleeping giants, and they're so far away and removed from God's ideal.

Many Christians have no understanding or concept of what Jesus taught. Many Christians know Jesus by name, but they don't know

Jesus. They don't personally know him. They don't have a personal relationship with Jesus Christ. They can't tell what Jesus is thinking. They can't tell what Jesus thinks about their life and their lifestyle. They have no understanding of the thoughts of Jesus. They're practically drowning in their wealth. They have so much wealth. They do not need anything, and they are practically asleep.

God desires his people to be awake and vigilant and be an influence and a light for this generation. God desires his people to be a witness, save souls, and influence the non-Christian community. So often, people in the Christian church do not affect unbelievers. This is a sad situation.

We need speakers and events to wake the church up.

Question 26: What does Jesus feel for people caught in addictions?

As I have previously shared, I lived with many addictions and lived for 40 years caught in addiction. Jesus was very nice to me.

I have three books where I encourage people to do their first personal prophecy over my life. I pray for people in those three books to receive the gift of prophecy and encourage them to practice their gift on me. Over many years since those books have been out, I've received hundreds of prophecies.

Jesus has repeatedly said in those prophecies that he's proud of me and loves me.

Can you imagine him saying that hundreds of times to a person caught in addiction? Can you imagine Jesus not only saying that he loves me as a person but he's proud of me? You may not be able to fathom that! You may not understand that Jesus can say many times that he was proud of me during my addicted life.

Jesus is a remarkable Savior. He's a wonderful person. He looks past our values; he looks past our faults and our sins, and he looks upon us as a person. He looks to our hearts. He looks to the purity of our hearts. He loves us as a person. He doesn't love the external. He doesn't look at the external; he forgives, loves, and encourages.

Jesus has encouraged me, and I've grown close to him. Even during my sinful life, he has been a God who has encouraged, blessed, and led me into a place of intimacy with himself. He has always encouraged me, built me up, and lifted my spirits.

It's contrary to how Christians speak of you and how religious Christians treat you. You're treated more as an outcast if you're sinning, and if you're in habitual sin, you are rejected and judged by religious Christians. However, Jesus especially loves you when you're in habitual sin. He delights in you, encourages you, and blesses you with the things that he has to say.

I think you'd have to be in habitual sin and be in a place where you're sinning regularly to experience the love of Jesus as I've experienced. I hope this was encouraging, especially if you're caught in a sin cycle.

Question 27: Can God use a person who is in sin?

I can answer that question based on my life, an addictive sin life that I've had. God has been using me in the last twelve years to write many Christian books, and he has used me to prophesy individuals' lives. God has certainly been using me.

We hear accounts of people caught in adultery, embezzling money, or other situations. Up until the day they were caught and exposed, God was using them.

We understand people in the Bible, sinful people, were used by God. We have the account of the apostle Paul killing Christians and putting Christians to death. He was arrested by God, thrown off his horse by Jesus, and then used. Though, he didn't continue in sin.

The Bible encourages us to live free of sin, but God can use sinners. He can use people caught in sin and live a life involving sin. This is not my way of saying to you that you should continue in your life of sin.

I suppose that it is very good for Jesus to be kind to people who aren't whole, to us people who are broken, and to help and encourage others who are broken.

I'm encouraged and blessed that Jesus has seen fit to use me to write 86 books. He's used my books to encourage thousands of people. I've been the person who has contributed to many sins in my life and been responsible for quite a lot of sins, and God has seen fit to use me. I believe many people have an addiction to pornography or an addiction to prostitutes that God is currently using. We live and serve a God of grace and mercy. He sees fit to us; broken individuals like me. A certain joy can be found in ministering and being used in ministry.

Some people would say, "If you've got sin in your life, you shouldn't be ministering. You shouldn't be doing personal prophecy over people." God has seen fit for me to be used in that way, and he's seen fit for me to write Christian nonfiction books to encourage people and bless people, and I believe it has given me something to live for and fill a purpose in my life. God has been by my side, encouraging and blessing me throughout the journey.

I pray that this chapter has encouraged you if you live with sinful things. I hope that this has been used to encourage you.

Question 28: Can someone be anointed and in sin?

Once again, the answer to that is yes. The gifts and the callings of God are without repentance, the Bible says. Just because someone is in sin doesn't mean their gifts get taken away. If they've got a calling, they can participate in it.

People who read my books report to me that their page-turners and that there is an anointing and presence of the Holy Spirit in my books. I'm aware that in my life, I have an anointing to teach and have an anointing on my prophecies.

I prophesied over a famous Christian who's got a big reputation in the world. She wrote an email to me saying that the prophecy I did for her was very anointed. I've had someone who's anointed and popular in the world say I've got an anointing.

In one of the letters of John, it says that "The Holy Spirit carries the anointing in our lives." When we have been anointed, we get the power to do a job from the Holy Spirit. Sometimes, sin in your life doesn't affect the anointing in your life. You get an anointing by the Holy Spirit, which is the power to do a job. The Holy Spirit can use people to minister to people, bless people, encourage people, and teach people. The Holy Spirit will rest on a person, even if they have sinned.

As I shared in the previous teaching, people who fall from grace, caught in adultery, embezzlement, or some major sin, ministered until the day they were caught. The anointing of God was resting on their life and could be used to minister up until they got discovered and exposed.

If you're struggling with something that is a sin in your life, God can still use you and effectively use you to touch, minister, and encourage people.

I am unsure what I would do if Jesus took my ability to minister from me. If God sidelined everyone with a measure of sin, there'd be no one to minister. That sounds a little extreme, but we all struggle with certain things. I'm so glad that the Holy Spirit has chosen to anoint me even though I've struggled with sin.

Please don't take what I have shared here as me endorsing a life of sin. It serves everyone best if you can free yourself from your sinful life through the grace of God. However, I am saying that until you are spotless, God can still use you effectively until that time comes.

Question 29: Did Jesus say a believer can go to hell?

Jesus was recorded in the Gospels, "If you don't forgive your brother, neither will I forgive you." If Jesus hasn't forgiven you, your sin isn't forgiven, and you'll end up in hell.

Jesus taught the narrow way. Jesus says, "Narrow is the way that leads to life, and few find that. But broad is the way that leads to destruction" Destruction is another word for hell. Some people wrongly imagine they are on a narrow path because they have decided to follow Jesus. However, Jesus' way is narrow.

You can look at my three books on the narrow way for more information on that, I've got a book on the parables of Jesus and what they mean. I've got a book on the commandments of Jesus and how to follow them. I've also got another book on the narrow way. I've got a series on the narrow way that will teach you how to be on the narrow way.

Jesus said, in Matthew 7, "Depart from me, you who practice lawlessness, I never knew you." Jesus was saying that to people who spoke in tongues, people who did signs and wonders, healings, prophesied, and did miracles. There is a type of Christian you can be, be a believer, and be sent to hell.

There are about ten parables that Jesus shares, where if you don't do the right thing, you'll end up in hell. Those parables were said to his disciples, who were his followers.

I've got a book called *The Parables that Disqualify you from going to Heaven*. I'd encourage you to read that book. Missing out on going to heaven is only an error away. Having the ability to go to heaven is a privilege.

Jesus is insistent in his parables. In one, he teaches about the person who was let go of a big debt and then took his servant and imprisoned him because he owed a smaller debt. He was caught by the person who forgave his debt, and he threw him into prison with the torturers, and torturers are a symbol of hell.

Jesus taught the parable of the sheep, and the goats, where the sheep went to heaven and the goats went to eternal torment. To be a sheep, you need to be a person who has mercy, forgives people's debts, feeds the hungry, waters the thirsty, and visits people in prisons and hospitals. Being a sheep is being a good-hearted person.

I can say that the sheep and the goat's parable identify the sort of person who deserves to go to heaven. I believe personally, as I've shared, that people who've never heard the Gospel will be judged by the sheep and goat's parable.

Many instances in Jesus' parables warn people about a lifestyle they must live to go to heaven.

Just saying a sinners' prayer and going to church on Sunday doesn't guarantee you are getting to heaven. You've got to live your life on the narrow way, and you've got to be seen, to be doing the will of God with your life and not just living your religious life.

I pray that this teaching has blessed you.

Question 30: Does witchcraft hold spiritual truth and realities?

I know a little bit about witchcraft; I don't know, a tremendous amount. But everything true in witchcraft, everything that works in witchcraft, comes from the Spirit of God. Every reality they minister in everything they do has a spiritual foundation in the things of God.

Witches can prophesy and do personal prophecies and can be accurate about things about your life and things about your future. They can prophesy correctly and accurately and use familiar spirits or other spirits called spirit guides to do what they do.

As a person who does personal prophecy, I would agree that although witchcraft uses a different spirit, it would be able to encourage and bless and minister to people, albeit in the wrong spirit. It isn't necessarily good for you to go through a clairvoyant, psychic, or witch to have your future prophesied, but it does happen.

Another thing about witchcraft is they can do what is called astral traveling; they can travel to a different location with their spirit and encounter people and situations where they're away from their bodies.

In Christian circles, that's called "Traveling in the Spirit." It's done a little differently, but it's the same thing. Some people travel in the spirit, quite often, sometimes with the whole body. I travel in the spirit when I visit heaven.

I know a person called Michael Van Vlymen who's travelled in his whole body, gone with his flesh body, to another country, from America, in a split second. He's encountered someone over there, done something, and then returned to the United States. Witches can do that; they can make astral travel, both in spirit and in their body. They can do the same thing.

Another similar thing, witchcraft, is the ability to contact the dead, and that is done through a medium or a witch, and they can contact dead relatives. Now, sometimes or many times, the dead person that speaks is a familiar spirit, a spirit that knows the deceased family and pretends to be the deceased. It's not a good thing to go to a medium.

I confess that I can speak to my parents, who passed away four years ago and three years ago. I speak to my parents daily in heaven and ask them what they're up to. We discuss my life on Earth. I've been used to bring messages from thirty saints in heaven to earth. I've recorded interviews with saints from Heaven in books I've produced. I must say that the people in heaven are alive in Christ and not dead or in hell. I can't contact people in hell under any circumstance.

As a spiritual reality, much that's available in witchcraft is also available to Christians. There are just three areas I know about that I participate in that are like witchcraft. I'd have to do a study of witchcraft to know more. Witches can read people's minds. I have been able to read minds from time to time. There are many similarities in witchcraft that there are in Christian circles. One of them is dark and dangerous, and one of them is light and righteous.

Witches are spiritual people, and they have real realities. The things that exist just because it is witchcraft doesn't mean it doesn't exist; it doesn't mean that they are not true, and it's just in darkness. I encourage you to be a friend to witches and put your arm around them and show them the love of God, and perhaps, the power in you may be able to attract them to convert.

I pray that this little teaching has blessed you and opened your eyes.

Question 31: Can teaching supported by Scripture still lead you astray?

As I mentioned in this book, I was led astray by what people would call a legalistic doctrine. This is a doctrine of holiness and sanctification, which is true, but with heavy-handedness with Scripture, weighing you down and making you feel condemned and guilty before the Lord.

The people with a legalistic doctrine try to serve an angry God of the Old Testament, a God of rules and regulations. You never seem to measure up under a legalistic doctrine. You are called to pray, but how many hours do you pray? People are left feeling condemned for not praying, not reading the Bible, and not worshiping enough.

It's a doctrine that's heavily based on doing good works. How many are enough good works? How much is needed? When you're not saved, by grace, when the love of Jesus does not save you, Legalistic doctrine can be supported by many Scriptures, as many Scriptures in the Bible can support that way of teaching, and Hyper Hyper-Grace, an extreme grace doctrine can also be supported by the Scripture.

You can have grace teachers teach and go so far as to say that you don't need to obey the teachings of Jesus. Hyper-Grace teachers will say that Jesus was teaching the law, and we are saved from the law. They say that you don't have to obey the teachings of Jesus. Jesus himself said that people would be considered the least in the Kingdom of God and would teach people not to obey the law. Jesus knew the Hyper-Grace; people were going to come. People who teach extreme grace support everything they must bring forth with Scripture verses.

People who teach legalistic works-based doctrine use many Scripture verses to teach what they teach, and people who teach extreme grace and Hyper-Grace use many Scripture verses to support what they say.

These doctrines on both sides cherry-pick Scriptures to support what they're saying. So, you can be led astray by teaching that seems to be supported by Scripture.

It's up to the Holy Spirit to help you to discern the truth in everything. I started legalistically, got saved by grace or doctrine, and then moved into Hyper-Grace and saw that they were talking about disobeying Jesus, and I came back to settle sort of in the middle but on the grace side of legalism.

I hope that this chapter encourages you.

Question 32: Is the church overrun by religion?

I'm not sure that anyone sets out with a course for their life to be religious. I think modern teaching in the pulpits teaches people to become religious and bound up with religion. I remember Jesus said, "The letter kills, but the Spirit gives life."

My understanding of the Scripture says that Jesus said the Bible doesn't bring life alone. It's just the Word of God, and it can bring death. But the Rhema Word, The Holy Spirit, inspired Word of God, brings life. I notice people who are religious-minded, who comment on my YouTube and make book reviews of my books. On Amazon, they are heavy with the number of Scriptures they quote. Religious people have that in common: they have many Bible verses that they tend to quote, and they tend to live by, and Jesus' words, saying that "The letter kills but the Spirit gives life," give some credence to what they do. Jesus preached and shared a message to encourage people to live as he prospered.

Jesus had 50 commandments for people to take on board and follow. Jesus had 54 parables, where he shared the way to live and the proposed way that he set down to live, and Jesus hoped through his 50 commandments and his 54 parables to show people how to live the proper Christian life. Jesus brought his Spirit to live within people and for them to live a life that demonstrates his life.

Jesus was not religious, and even though He had 50 commands, they were rules for life. They were ways of expressing your love for people and your love for God. People have left that aside and don't want to live the life that Jesus showed us in his teaching. Instead, they go to church, sing songs, listen to sermons, and read the Bible, religiously. They consider that the Bible verses will set them free, and they live this rigid, detailed life of good works. They never seem to measure up. They have all these rules for life that they impose upon themselves, and they mistakenly impose those rules upon others. The church, by and large, has become a place of rigidity, where there's not a lot of freedom to move and express oneself.

Sadly, it's become overrun by religion. Only the Spirit of the Lord and the interpretation of the Holy Spirit on the Word of God bring freedom, and it's the Holy Spirit, through his intervention in our lives, that brings freedom. Sadly, many people in the religious church haven't been baptized in the Holy Spirit.

There's a measure of the power of the Holy Spirit that is active in some of these people's lives, and because of that, they become free and abandon religion.

Question 33: Is Satan powerful or defeated?

According to my life and my experiences, I would have to answer that Satan is powerful. I know there are Scriptures and people who believe Satan is under our feet and Satan is a defeated foe. But in my life, he has had an effect through temptation, speaking to and harassing me. He is a force to be reckoned with.

When you consider your enemy has no power or influence, or feel that you can be influenced more, I sense that it is a wiser approach to life, to credit your enemy with their power.

Through the Gospel message and the Word of God, I understand that Satan is a roaring lion who seeks who he can devour. If you're not fully aware of his devices, you can succumb to his power; you can succumb to his influence.

This is one of the reasons why it says that We should put on the full armor of God and stand and fight the fight.

I have had, on many occasions, Satan speak to me or a lesser demon, pretending to be him, speaking to me, and taunting me. I'm fully aware that I have a mental illness and a schizophrenic ability to hear voices. I'm aware that the average Christian probably hasn't received the reception levels, so I must. Satan has influenced my life. He's used his influence to keep me in a life of sin, and it's had a destructive impact on my life.

Because of that, I don't consider Satan to be defeated in my life. I'm ever vigilant to fight the good fight of faith. I know that each time I publish a book, I get a sense that I am delivering Satan or a knockout blow as hundreds of people orders my book in the first month after its publication. I consider myself delivering Satan or knockout blow and having him hit the canvas, but I live a troubled life and can have many tribulations and trials. My life would be a lot different if Satan didn't exist, so I don't consider Satan defeated in my life, although Scripture and famous teachers may disagree with me.

I pray that this has encouraged you.

Question 34: Can an ordinary Christian heal people?

I would consider myself quite ordinary as a Christian. I live a somewhat supernatural life. I wouldn't consider myself officially trained in the fivefold ministry. I wasn't someone who's been to seminary or Bible school. I consider myself quite ordinary. God has used me to heal people two times. One time, I had a woman that was part of my prophetic ministry, ministry team, and we used to do prophetic words for people. One day she wrote to me and said to me, asking me to pray for her. She said that she had had a migraine that lasted for seven years, and it's hard to organize her daughter and get through the day with this powerful migraine hurting her. She said for me to get an idea of how much pain she was in, she told me a story. She said she had a car accident while she had her migraine. She was given some morphine tablets for her back pain due to the injury in the car accident. She said the morphine tablets took the back pain away. However, the strength of the tablets didn't touch the pain in the migraine, and it persisted while she took morphine tablets. I didn't have the faith to heal her.

The next day, I caught a train. As I got off the train, I started to cry. As my heart went out to this woman, I asked the Lord to heal her and not have her migraine return; I opened an email when I got to my place. I typed, "I prayed for God to heal your migraine, and I pray that my prayer will be effective."

The next day, she said, she opened an email, and the power of God hit her and knocked her to the floor. When she got up off the floor, her migraine had gone.

So here I am, a normal Christian with no supernatural powers, and I was used to healing a migraine. I had known her for several years after that event, and her migraine stayed away.

I was also used once with a person who had chronic back pain. Jesus told me to pray for him. I prayed for his back, which was miraculously healed at that time, and for years afterward, his back was fine.

So, the Lord has used me two times to heal. In answer to this question, I feel that ordinary Christians can be raised by Jesus and used to heal people. Jesus said in the Great Commission that Christians would be up to heal, and it's possible.

I've got a friend who's written a book called *Divine Healing Made Simple,* which instructs you and teaches you to heal. He's had a lot of success as a teacher; many people have read his book and gone on to heal.

I want to encourage you that the Spirit of God within you can be used to heal people and bring people into wholeness. I pray that you are encouraged by this short teaching.

Question 35: Can an ordinary Christian prophesy?

I remember, thirty years ago, I used to drive a taxi and have passengers in a taxi. From time to time, Jesus gave me a message for one of my customers, and I'd share with the customer what Jesus was saying. This was me using personal prophecy. That's essentially all it is. You can hear what he says if you have a relationship with Jesus.

You can be used to prophesy; Jesus can tell you something to tell a person, it doesn't have to be earth-shattering. It doesn't have to be mind-blowing. It can just be something encouraging, a word about their personality that Jesus loves. Or something about their behavior that Jesus loves.

Jesus is the most encouraging entity in the universe. He has wonderful things to say. As a Christian, your life can be enriched if Jesus uses you as a vessel to prophesy and bring people words of edification and encouragement.

You can read a book on prophecy. I've got a book called *Prophetic Evangelism Made Simple*. It explains the gift of prophetic evangelism. It also explains giving people who are strangers on the streets prophecies, and at the end of the book, it has a prayer for you to pray to receive the gift of prophecy. Then it has an exercise for you to write me an email and prophesy over me. When I receive those emails, I read the prophecies and write feedback on your first prophecy. Then what you do with that gift is the practice of prophesying to people in your church. It's as simple as asking Jesus for a message for someone in your church, and he'll give you a name.

You get a piece of paper or get your keyboard out and type out the message that Jesus would have us say to a person and print it out and take it to church with you. You say to a person. "You were on my mind today, and Jesus gave me a message for you." Then you pass it on to them. You can even take the message to your pastor and let him read it before you pass the note on.

I encourage you to get the book *Prophetic Evangelism Made Simple*, pray the prayer, and enter a life of prophecy. I've done about 20,000 prophecies, and I'm encouraged each time someone writes to my ministry and requests a personal prophecy. You also can be used to prophesy and lift people's lives and encourage people.

I hope you're blessed by this message.

Question 36: Do false prophets start as true prophets?

I only know one person, personally, that I would categorize as a false prophet. From listening to her, you would ascertain that she loves the Lord Jesus, yet she's leading many people astray with what she teaches and shares.

I spoke about her in an earlier chapter, where I said I knew another person who could talk about this lady's encounters for two hours. She would share story after story that this prophet has shared. If I let it go, she could go on and on, sharing story after story for two hours.

I asked this friend of mine, "Do you think you could share the teachings of Jesus for two hours straight? Do you think you could share the teachings of Jesus for an hour? Could you share with me what Jesus taught for an hour?"

My friend wondered why I was asking the question and said, "No," she couldn't share the teachings of Jesus for an hour.

I said, "Well, this, this prophet, has become a false prophet to you because you can share what she shared for two hours straight. But you can't share what Jesus taught. She has become an idol. She has become a false god to you, leading you astray with her teachings."

The people who listened to this woman were addicted to her. I called the people junkies; they had to have their daily fix. They had to have the daily injection of what this woman shared. The people were very loyal.

I don't do videos doing this anymore, but I did a video exposing some of the false teachings that this prophet did. Spiritual witchcraft attacked me, which sent me to the hospital in an ambulance with my heart going out of place. It wasn't until the hospital that a hospital put the monitors on me and said to me, "There was nothing wrong with my heart." It wasn't until then that the spell broke. But that witchcraft came from her followers, praying prayers against me because I spoke up.

A false prophet has an anointing, just like I shared in these teachings, that you can be anointed and in sin. The gifts of God are irrevocable once you have the anointing of God. The gifts of God remain in your life, and you can go off the path and start to teach something that's not right and lead the people that are following you astray, and you still have the spiritual anointing. You'll still have the spiritual power you would have if you were a true prophet, and you could become a false prophet and still have the spiritual power.

False prophets have started the ministry, they start their life as true prophets, and then they go astray. I pray that you are encouraged and learn something in this teaching.

Question 37: Can anyone be led to teach and anointed to do so?

It says in one John, the letter of 1 John, that we're all anointed by the Holy Spirit. Those of us who are born again are anointed by the Holy Spirit. It says we need no one to teach us, but the Holy Spirit will teach us. There is an office in the fivefold ministry of teaching. I believe there's also a teaching gift and an ability to teach, and it may not be supported by Scripture, but I believe anyone can be used to teach Christian or non-Christian.

You can be used when you live a life with many questions and diligently seek the Lord for the answers to your questions. You can live a life with many questions in your mind, and having a question answered gives you an opportunity to share that answer with other people. You may choose to do a YouTube video with an answer to the question like this YouTube video. You may choose to post the answer to the question on Facebook. Or you might choose, like most people, choose to keep the answer to yourself and not share the answer with other people.

I sense that everyone who has questions about the Kingdom of God is constantly reading books, seeing posts, reading things in the Word of God, hearing supernaturally from Jesus, and getting constant answers to their questions. This gives people multiple opportunities to share their answers with people. I feel that a regular person like myself can be used to teach people and be given the power to share their discoveries with other people.

I sense that Jesus would enjoy more people, like yourself, teaching the mysteries of God, teaching the secrets of God, and teaching the fundamentals of the Kingdom to other people.

I ask you, dear reader, to consider starting a blog, sharing your answers to questions with others, and doing a weekly blog post. I ask you to consider sharing the answers you're finding through your questions on Facebook and sharing it with others. Perhaps start a YouTube channel and share the answers to your questions.

I know that the Holy Spirit is a teacher, and I know that the Holy Spirit can give you different levels of anointing and power to share answers and to share Kingdom truths with other people.

I'm sure that The Holy Spirit would give you the power to share the answers to the questions you may be getting. I sense that everyone can teach.

In the early church, they used to meet in home groups. As people were inspired, they would share a message with the other people in the home group. The Holy Spirit would come upon people with a message to share. We've moved away from that and put pastors and important people in the pulpits. We've moved away from people, sharing in small groups what the Holy Spirit has placed on their hearts.

The same dynamic exists today, and you, as a little person in the kingdom of God, can receive a message you can share with others.

I pray that this has encouraged you and you can be encouraged to share your message with other people.

Question 38: Has everyone got something worthwhile to teach?

Following on from our previous chapter, I say that everyone has questions. They've got questions about certain things in the Bible, certain passages in the Bible, certain concepts in the Bible, certain concepts about Christianity and their faith.

Many people have questions about life and success, and love. Out of all these questions, we find that everyone has something positive that they can teach.

I guess it comes down to whether you feel confident to teach something. I know that Facebook has allowed people to become more expressive, and YouTube has allowed people to express themselves; thousands of people on YouTube do small teachings and thousands of people have a blog posts. Many people are expressing themselves. My question to you is, why can't you be one of them?

My question to you is, what's holding you back from sharing some truth that you've come to realize you've come to understand? The Holy Spirit desires people to speak forth truth, to bring the truth out into the open. You may be a person who's a critical thinker, you may be a person that weighs information up in a correct way, who's very discerning of truth and discerning of what's right and wrong, and you can share that. You may be a person who has a unique perspective on why people enjoy your stories and people enjoy listening to you. You may be a person who attracts people's attention when you speak up.

Everyone has something worthwhile to say, and everyone can be used to teach the body of Christ. Sometimes I wish that more common people would speak up. Today we have the realm of self-publishing that has opened, and Amazon books have allowed people to self-publish their books. People are welcome to write a book, put a good cover on it, write a good description for the back cover, upload the book, and teach people and expand people's knowledge.

God delights in leading people and having them say something worthwhile for people to hear. Everyone is part of the body; everyone has a part to play. You'll find that you have worthwhile things to say. You could encourage the body of Christ.

So, take a chance, take the opportunity to step out on Facebook and write a post or start a free blog and start to blog your thoughts and encourage people and bless him.

I believe that everyone has good information to share and has certain knowledge and truths that the world could do with.

I encourage you to take a step today to make a difference. Take a step today to share your knowledge with people.

Question 39: Do books on people's life stories sell well?

I've written 86 books at present. The book on my life sells about the fifth lowest out of the 86 books. I have 86 books that share different teachings of Jesus and share different aspects of the Kingdom of God, and they are all better sellers than the book of my life.

You would imagine by the time someone has 86 books that, they're well known, and the people who are reading my books would come to be fascinated with my life and want to learn more about my life as an author and go on to read my life story; and in some cases, that happens. But the book remains to be one of my lowest sellers.

People generally are not interested in a person's life unless they are a famous person who has done famous things. Think about it, do you read the self-published book of one of your friends? Or do you read a properly published book by a Hollywood star or some movie star?

I am aware that if most people consider that one day, they'll write a book, they have the idea to write a book about their life. They consider that that's the only book that they can write. They consider writing a book on their own life. I'm afraid to tell you, to be honest, your book on your own life isn't going to sell well. You're not going to have a lot of people download your book and read your book.

I've found that even people I know don't read my books; it's mostly strangers, and how are strangers ever going to find your book and find out that you have a book when they don't even know who you are?

If you have bipolar disorder, as I do, and schizophrenia, you may write a book about the lessons you've learned from your life with bipolar disorder.

"10 Tips to Managing Bipolar and Having a Successful Life despite it" would be a good title for a book. In that book, I could go into a lot of detail about my life and the struggles I've had with my life.

Someone who has a loved one who has bipolar or someone who has bipolar would possibly be interested in a book about 10 tips to overcome bipolar and have a successful life. Even people who want a successful life may be interested in that book.

If you're thinking of writing a book about your life, consider writing a book, "10 Ways to Have an Overabundant Life as a Housewife," and you could write about a housewife. Still, you could write about 10 factors that make you a super achiever, a good mother, and a good housekeeper. What makes you a good manager of money? What makes you a good cook?

If you're thinking of writing a book, and you want to write a book about your life, consider the readers, consider giving readers something to benefit from your book, something that stands out and something that will teach them something, rather than just the book about your life story.

I'm sure you can include your life story in the book, and each of your 10 points can be illustrated by stories from your life and the lessons you learn from each of those stories. If the book has a theme outside of your life and something people can grab hold of and learn from, it will be a better book. As I said, I've got a book about my life, but it's a very low seller. Parts of me are in every book that I write. As you've read this book, you have realized that I lean heavily on my testimony, and parts and different glimpses of my life can be seen in the answers to each of these questions. So too, it can happen with your book on your life.

Question 40: Do guardian angels see your sin?

I had that question on my list of questions to ask in this book and for me to answer in this book, and I just asked my guardian angel for the answer. Has my guardian angel seen me visit prostitutes? Has my guardian angel seen me masturbate to porn? Has my guardian angel been a witness to my sin? My guardian angel says yes, he has seen me in all the hundreds of times I've done it. It's part of his duty to inspire me and encourage me out of my life of sin. He understands me, and he understands my struggle. He understands me as a person through witnessing my sin.

You may be surprised that you have a cloud of witnesses in heaven who witness your life and can see the sins you commit outside of your guardian angel. That may give you pause when you attempt or come across a time when you're going to sin. You may be a person who's very gifted and blessed with the gift of gossip. You may be very experienced in sharing stories about other people's lives. You can be sure that your guardian angel is a witness to those times when you gossip and break God's laws

The guardian angel sees a lot and your guardian angel prays for you to overcome, and your guardian angel gives you alternate thoughts about your cause of action and when you're going to attempt to sin. When you've decided to sin, your guardian angel will sometimes give you an alternate thought and course of action to stop you from your destructive path. It's good to know that heaven sees your life and not an edited version of your life. The more your guardian angel sees you participate in sin, the more invested they become in your life, and the more they can understand and empathize with you. The more they can be used to direct you with good thoughts and good plans for your life. Your guardian angel isn't embarrassed when they see your sin. It's more of a thought of understanding you and more for them to consider plans and methods to get your behavior changed and liberated. They live and breathe for your liberation and pray for and encourage you with thoughts to pursue a different path. This is one of the things that your guardian angel does. They love you. They pray for you, on your side and in your corner. It's like our boxer has a coach in his corner that he returns to. Your guardian angel is like a coach in your corner, helping you pursue the fire of life and Christian life.

I pray that this encourages you.

Question 41: What jobs do guardian angels do?

Guardian angels do more than protect you, guardian angels can protect you and keep you out of harm, but they also have seen your whole life played out. They've watched a movie about your future life in heaven, and they constantly give you thoughts to direct you to the will of God in your life. Guardian angels put thoughts in your mind to direct you. Your guardian angel may want you to go down to the shopping center because there's going to be a person down there that heaven wants you to interact with. Like the Holy Spirit, the guardian angel will put a thought in your mind to go shopping now and not later in the afternoon, and you'll get this urgency to go down the shops.

Your brother, who lives with you, as my brother lives with me, may ask you, "Are you going down the shops now? Can you get something for me?"

It turns out that you're at the shopping center in one of the isles where you're getting the shopping for your brother. You may bump into the person that the guardian angel wanted you to see so they can direct you and guide you to having divine encounters. They can organize your day for you. When you get back from the shops, they can have things organized for you to do for the rest of the day.

Guardian angels are involved when you go online to search for a book, that the guardian angel may give you the search words to type into Amazon to search for a certain book, and they'll highlight the book to you. Your sight will see a book and be attracted to the book. They will help you choose a book heaven wants you to buy. That will also lead you to look at the portion on Amazon that says:

People who bought these books also bought these books. You may be looking for a book and come across that section on Amazon. Rather than purchasing the book you found, you may go to that page and find another book the angel wants you to read. You may also be led to the author page of the author who wrote a book you found yourself looking at. You may get this inspiration in your thoughts to look at the author page, and you might get to the author page and find another book that the guardian angel wants you to read.

You can be directed through websites, and your guardian angel can direct you. You can look for a YouTube video on a certain subject and click on a YouTube video. There may be videos that your eyes may go to the suggested videos, and your eyes may be attracted to a certain video, and it turns out to be a video that your guardian angel wants you to see.

So, guardian angels can direct you and guide you. You can be down and not feel encouraged and feeling depressed, and your guardian angel can put good thoughts in your mind and encouraging thoughts. Your guardian angel can inspire you to do certain things that change your mood. Your guardian angel can play good memories with you and recite Scripture verses or recite songs to you and sing songs that lift your spirits and change your mood. Your guardian angel acts like the Holy Spirit and works in tandem with the Holy Spirit. Your guardian angel will give you good thoughts towards the person with whom the guardian angel wants you to make a friendship. Your guardian angels will lead you in so many different areas.

I've got a book that covers messages from people's guardian angels, and you can choose to look up that book and read the guardian angels' messages and get more of an idea of what guardian angels do.

Question 42: Is it possible to have multiple angels in your life?

Is it possible to have multiple angels in your life? I'll answer that, according to myself. Yes, it is possible to have multiple angels being used in your life.

I have, personally, a guardian angel called "*Michael*," who is my guardian angel and does many things for me but also is a prophetic angel that administers my prophetic gift and anoints me with the power to do prophetic words.

I also have an angel called "*Bethany*," a scribe angel. Bethany will inspire titles for books and inspire me to write chapter titles, which become the foundation of any book I write. Bethany will inspire me to do Facebook posts and inspire me to do YouTube videos and inspire the title of the Facebook posts and the title of YouTube videos. Bethany inspires me and uses her intellect and understanding to give me the words to say in my books and give me the words to say in my YouTube videos, and my Facebook posts.

Bethany is used with a famous writer in the past, and she allowed him to be prolific, but I won't give you his name. I felt privileged and honored to have Bethany as my scribe Angel.

I've got an angel called "*Mark*," who works with finances. He's my finance, Angel. He puts it in the hearts of people to give towards my ministry. He puts it in people's hearts to request prophecies and sends me donations on PayPal. He inspires people to buy my books, which earn me finances, and he looks after my finances. He even helps me choose workers who will help me publish my books. He leads me to cheaper options and cheaper alternatives with contractors that work in my life.

I've got an Angel called "*Elisha*," who will be used in the future to organize speaking engagements and to organize my anointing when it comes to preaching on Revival. At present, he organizes the other angels in my life.

I've got multiple angels, and it's possible to have multiple angels in your life that all do our specific duty. Elisha organizes as my angels, and as seen doing what they are called to do, you get more angels depending on how busy you are fulfilling the role of your life, and however busy you are working in the Kingdom will determine how many angels are part of your life.

I highly use Bethany, and my guardian angel is highly used to direct and sustain me through my life. They lead me to do many books and videos. You might be aware that I have produced 86 books, and I need a lot of input coming into my life to give me the material and foundation for me to preach on many subjects.

I pray that this has helped you and encouraged you.

Question 43: Can you be a friend of God like Abraham?

Abraham inspires us to behold and follow God and do things according to God's will and purposes. We all know that Abraham was called away from his family and wealth. Abraham went and ventured and followed the Lord into the unknown.

Life can be a bit of an unknown reality to us. Life can be tough and unfair. We need to know that we can draw close to the Lord and our Father in heaven and have an intimate relationship with him.

Part of drawing close to God was found for me in writing personal journals to God. I wrote a journal on my computer to God and did a series of books called "*Conversations with God*" It was named after a book called "Conversations with God" by another author, which sold millions of copies. I chose the same title because that's what I was having, conversations with God.

In my series of Conversations with God, I drew close to him, like you would draw close to a friend, having conversations with a friend. The more questions I asked, and God spoke, the clearer our friendship was defined.

I encourage you, as a Christian, to get out of your computer and start a journal with God. Start to write down what you want to say to God, write down questions for God, and write down God's responses and answers to your questions.

It is possible to develop a close and intimate relationship with God; God doesn't have to be someone distant in the clouds on a throne that never interacts with you. He doesn't need to be an angry god that looks at you and judges everything that you do with a harsh penalty. He doesn't need to be some far away God, but he can speak personally to you in a journal or speak into your mind as thought as you talk back and forth to him.

I have a book on how to have conversations with God. I encourage you to order that book and read that book and develop a conversational style of speaking to him.

God lives in heaven and desires to be friends with people on Earth. He's got so much to say. He's got so many feelings and so many emotions, and he looks for people on earth to draw close to him and become his friend. You can become his confidant. You can become someone to whom he pours his heart and shares his emotions.

In my book, "*Conversations with God Book 3,*" God gets emotional in what he says. You can read that book and see that God is a personable God. God is a humble God. Although he's an all-powerful God, he can be understood, reasoned with, and heard in a humble way. God has so much that he wants to share with you, and he wants to encourage you in your life and your Christian life, and he wants to come alongside you and be your friend. I pray that this has blessed you.

Question 44: Does God want more friends?

God is different from normal human beings. A normal human being can only converse with one person at a time. They can have an audience of people and speak to an audience, and they can't speak to a hundred people at once, but God is different. He can have a two-way conversation with millions of people at once. God can also have millions of friends and millions of people that love him. He can interact and dialogue with millions of people.

One thing I know about God is that he desires friendship; he desires intimate friendship with himself. God has so much on his mind, and it doesn't take you to be a prophet or a friend of God to hear from God. I believe a prophet, in essence, is a friend of God. Abraham was a friend of God; King David was a friend of God. Elijah was a friend of God. God can have special friends; however, he desires everyone to be his friend.

You can learn to draw closer to God by doing journals, as I suggested. You can learn to have two-way Conversations with God. Through two-way Conversations with God, you grow, get to know him, and grow in your intimacy. You can reach a stage where you can ask God questions, and God can answer your questions one by one. Sometimes, we're too afraid to ask God a question. Sometimes there are things in our life that are too emotional for us to ask God a question about them.

I know that I would ideally love a future wife. But I don't ask God questions about that. Sometimes, people prophesy and say that I have a wife coming.

God has real emotions and distress with what's happening in the world. God isn't always a happy God. What eternal Father would have so many distressed sons and daughters and remain unaffected by it? God gets affected by the suffering in the world, the trafficking of enslaved people on coffee plantations, the sex trafficking, the paedophilia, the sexual abuse; there are so many things that distress God and bring his countenance down. He desires friends who can understand him, friends he can talk to.

Sometimes it's good to talk to a friend and get things off your chest. Just talking to a friend and having them listen to you can be very therapeutic. You don't need your friend to necessarily have the answers to what you're going through. They don't have to have the solutions for you. But just the act of listening brings comfort and peace.

In that way, God needs people on Earth, people established on Earth with lives and influences to listen to him. He has a lot to say. So many people pray one-way prayers to God, fill God up with their requests, repent before God, and try to re-establish their relationship after they've sinned with God and have a litany of requests for God. But they don't stop and listen to God; they don't talk to God or have a two-way conversation with God. God gets distressed about that. He loves people that can have a two-way conversation with him. He wants people to listen to him, especially be there for him to unburden his heart with. If you desire to be a friend of God's like that, that will do God a lot of good, and I encourage you to work towards being a friend of God; God can certainly do with it.

Question 45: Can you be a prophet of God and not have a big ministry?

Can you be a prophet of God and not have a big ministry? I would say I qualify as a prophet of God. I have not got a very big ministry. So yes, it's possible to be a prophet of God and not have a big ministry. God desires friends and people to listen to him and help him with his emotional issues.

Sometimes, he doesn't need you to preach to thousands of people. Sometimes he doesn't need you to speak to thousands of people. Sometimes he wants to share his heart with you, just like a person can be a lone intercessor who takes situations and people before the throne room in prayer. People can be intercessors and not have a big reputation or big following. It's possible to be a friend of God and a prophet, and not have a big following and not have a major influence in the world.

Part of being a Christian and living in God's will is knowing your place and your station in life. Happiness truly comes from being who you're destined to become. You can have wonderful prophecies over your life, talking about having an international ministry and influencing thousands of people. You can wait for those prophecies to come true like I have been waiting for 42 years. You must become comfortable with the life that you're living; it's important that you can remain stable and not be depressed at the fact that you're just influencing a small number of people.

When you're a prophet and a friend of his, you can watch the news broadcast and get more out of it. You can be a friend of God, and God can give you the news behind the news. He can speak to you about politicians, he can speak to you about actors, he can speak to singers, and reveal the secrets of those people's hearts. He can have a two-way dialogue with you and share where the people are coming from and why they're saying what they're saying and what he thinks of them.

God can use you to be an intercessor and pray for people. God can highlight people to you and tell you the issues they're dealing with, and he can call you to pray and intercede for a person. God can use you via personal prophecy to touch people's lives and minister to people's lives. He can use you to do Facebook posts that are encouraging. He can use you to write books. He can use you to do videos and encourage people. God can use you as a prophet in so many ways. You don't have to be a household name. You don't have to appear on Sid Roth; you don't have to appear on popular television shows.

You can be just a simple Prophet who has an audience of God and who ministers to God's heart with his thoughts, intellect, emotions, and actions. You can be a prophet of God who ministers to God, and you can be a little person and be satisfied being a little person. You could write books that only sell a couple of monthly copies, like the books I write. You can be used in all ways by God, who sees everything and knows everything.

I pray that this chapter blesses you.

Question 46: Does God return tenfold for some giving?

We should never be seduced by the prosperity message that espouses that we give to be blessed. The blessings of God and the financial income we derive shouldn't be focused on our giving. We should give from joyful hearts and according to how the Holy Spirit ministers to our hearts and leads us with our hearts. We should not ever be given the desire to reap a return from God.

Our attitude to giving should be one birthed out of a good heart and a generous soul, and not be influenced by people who teach the prosperity doctrine, which says that if you want to be blessed by God, you should give your money into good soil. They say you should give your money to places assured of bringing your harvest and a financial return.

God loves a cheerful giver and people to give towards his purposes and ministries. So many Christian ministries depend on faithful giving. I admire the people who give monthly to my ministry and have become partners in giving to my small book publishing ministry. I appreciate the people that give to me, and the donations, even the small ones, make a difference in my life.

I have had times when I've given to the Lord and received a tenfold return. I remember one ministry I was following called *"Revival of Riots"* that I gave $25 donation to on one month and people over the following month gave me what added up to be $250 worth of income and resources. The next month, I gave $25; again, people gave me $250 worth of resources. I backed that ministry for three months at $25 a month. Then the ministry started to get into error and promote error. I withdrew my finance for that ministry. But for those three months, I gave a total of $75, and I received a return of $750.

Of course, if you're receiving a tenfold return on your finances, if you're receiving a tenfold return on your giving, you can give all day. You can give out of the abundance of return on your money. I have received a tenfold return multiple times in my life. I must stress that the Holy Spirit has always led me in my giving. I suggest you are led by the people God has called you to give to, and the Holy Spirit leads you on how much to give.

God desires that we give to his ministry. He likes us having a hands-off approach to money. He likes to use us to bless individuals and ministries, and he likes for us to be moved on by his Holy Spirit and directed and led by the Holy Spirit when it comes to giving. God can and will give you a tenfold return on your giving and bless you at times. I've had multiple times where I've given a ministry $50 and got a return of $500. Most often, I get a one-to-one return on my giving. This allows me to continue to give to ministries and continue to give to individuals, as I feel directed by the Holy Spirit.

God is not constrained to man's ideas and isn't controlled by what a man thinks. Some people in the prosperity doctrine talk about a tenfold return, and fiftyfold return hundredfold return and all things are possible with God. I encourage you, as someone who's got finances, to listen to the voice of the Holy Spirit, and give to the ministries and the people and individuals that the Holy Spirit directs you to give the amount that the Holy Spirit tells you to give them, in that way you can be assured that God will look after you when it comes to finances.

Question 47: Should we tithe today?

Many people will post on the internet, write articles, and make videos sharing that the tithe isn't required today. They say that in the New Testament, we're not required to tithe because it was said to be part of the law. These tithing laws were tied to the tribe of Levi, and they didn't give money but gave grain and produce to the tribe of Levi so they could survive.

So, many people teach, "we're not required to tithe today."

I understand that the law of giving and rewards is discussed in the Bible. The Bible spelled out the concept of giving and getting a return on your finances. I sense that if you're giving, according to the Holy Spirit, your giving would exceed the 10% tithe.

For 20 years, I have been giving about 25% of my income to the Lord. That's my income, and 100% of my ministry income goes back to the ministry. I sense that some people listen to the teaching and follow people that teach on the tithe and how it's not necessary today; I suspect some don't tithe 10% and give far less than 10%.

There's been a statistic that I've read regularly that says only 5% of Christians in the United States give a tithe. Another article said Christians in the States give about 2% of their income. So, 95% of Christians in the United States don't give a tithe.

It all comes down to what you think of God and ministry. Most of my extra income goes into producing books for people. My books are now free. Most of my books are 99 cents to buy on Kindle. Once every three months, I make all my books free. The books I'm producing now, for last 10 books I've produced, I've made permanently free on Amazon.

I work in a ministry to teach people, equip people, and encourage people in the things of the Lord, and all my finances, all my spare finances, go into producing books. I encourage you to seek the Lord on giving.

Michael Van Vlymen has a good book on financial stewardship called "Supernatural Provision: Learning to Walk in Greater Levels of Stewardship and Responsibility and Letting Go of Unbiblical Beliefs."

Andrew Wommack has a good book called "*Financial Stewardship.*" They encourage you to give as the Holy Spirit lays people and ministries on your heart to give to.

God is a rewarder, and God loves a cheerful giver. I encourage you to grow close to the Holy Spirit and reach a stage in your personal life where the Holy Spirit is directing you and when it comes to giving, be sensitive to the voice of the Holy Spirit.

I agree with the teachers that it's not necessary to tithe. I believe if you're following the leading of the Holy Spirit in your life, as the Holy Spirit wants to lead you, you will be giving far more than a tithe out of your income each week. I pray that this has been used to bless you and encourage you.

Question 48: Is the prosperity doctrine based on truth?

Many false doctrines, many doctrines that lead people astray, are based on scriptural proof. We've already discussed that the doctrine of legalism and the doctrine of Hyper-Grace, are based on scriptural references. You can use the Bible to support nearly anything you want to say. You can grab a collection of verses and support anything you want to say.

The prosperity doctrine, espoused by many teachers, is based on carnality. It's based on our lust for things for the world. Many people make a living by teaching the prosperity doctrine to live a carnal life. They live a life described by Jesus in the church of Laodicea, they live a life where they don't need God, and they've got no need for God, and they've got riches and wealth, and they have a lavish lifestyle.

The prosperity doctrine proponents will hear Jesus say, "Depart from me; I never knew you."

There are people with huge ministries and millions of dollars' worth of finances coming through their ministries, supported by the faulty and misleading doctrine that allows them to fleece gullible listeners for money.

The idea that you can prosper and become rich through giving is a vile doctrine and one that I would like to discourage. I have a book called "*Money- Money-Money*." In that book, I talk about the prosperity doctrine and how destructive it is.

Many false teachers and prophets propose and teach the prosperity doctrine. You'll find that there are a great many Scriptures in the Bible that support their teaching, just like legalism and Hyper-Grace, which are based on many Scriptures but can have you bound in error. So too, the prosperity doctrine is based on a lot of Scripture references.

James says in James 4:4, "Adulterers and adulteresses, don't you know that friendship with the world makes you at enmity with God, whoever therefore wants to become a friend of the world becomes an enemy of God."

Pursuing wealth, pursuing riches, and pursuing the earth's goods for yourself, which is what prosperity doctrine believers do, is living with the lust of the world and living in the world. It's becoming a friend of the world. According to James, this will put you in a position where you're not a friend of God. So, it's a dicey line. Many people who preach the prosperity doctrine will hear Jesus say, "Depart from me; I never knew you." They can be doing signs and wonders, prophesying, and doing miracles, and still be told they're going to hell. If you listen to these people, you follow these people, and you give to the Lord to get a return and be blessed financially, you could become a friend of the world and an enemy of God.

I encourage you to give as the Holy Spirit leads you and give to people that he encourages you to give to and consult with the Holy Spirit on how much to give and get away and stop listening to people who preach the prosperity message. I hope this has encouraged you.

Question 49: Can you teach error and still bless people?

Many churches preach a works and legalistic doctrine, and people who attend churches get weighed down by religious burdens and destruction. So many people who attend those churches are blessed. Some people attend churches that teach Hyper-Grace, and extreme grace doctrine, and those people you find very happy and feel very blessed.

You can indeed teach error and bless people.

The modern church is full of errors. So many people teaching the Word of God are in error. Some so many people listen to the Word of God, feel good and feel blessed, and are encouraged when the Word of God is preached, but are receiving and digesting errors. This is a sad thing, but a reality.

It takes dedication and a humble and teachable spirit to develop the ability to withdraw yourself from error and come to a proper understanding of many things.

I believe my life has seen different courses and meanderings. My life has not always been free of error. I believe my life is still affected by certain errors I'm unaware of. Many people attending churches worldwide are blessed, encouraged, inspired, and built up. Yet, what are they being taught, and what do they have to digest? Many times, there are errors.

If you talk to a hyper-grace teacher, the teacher fully believes in what they're teaching and wouldn't consider being called a false teacher or false prophet. If you were to interview a person who teaches legalistic doctrine and a works doctrine, you'd also understand that they believe that they're teaching the truth. They wouldn't believe they're being used to share falsity with everyone. Nearly everyone that is a teacher teaches, what they believe is truth, and they wouldn't understand unless it was highlighted by the Holy Spirit that they are teaching error.

It is important to understand that you can teach error and bless people, and people, through congregations, all around the world, are being lied to and taught error. They are blissfully unaware of that. They're full of bliss, happiness, prosperity, and enjoyment, unaware that what is being fed is a diet of miss truth and error.

I pray for you in this instance. I pray that the Holy Spirit may become intimate with you. I pray that you get a fresh revelation of the Word of God and that the Holy Spirit may lead you into all truth. I pray that you were blessed by this message and encouraged by it.

Question 50: Is there ever going to be unity in the church?

You can come across people who are enemies of each other and continue to have skirmishes within their families. You can bring in some foreign enemies to both families that are having skirmishes. When you bring our common enemy, the people having the skirmishes and fights will join and fight the common enemy and become one in unity as they fight off the common enemy.

I believe the church may come into unity in the last days as tribulation, and hardship comes to the church and the people in the world. I believe unity won't be achieved in the World Council of Churches. I don't believe human ideas and a one-world church will bring about unity in anything that tries to unify the world's religions; under one God is a false peace. This is a false unity. The Catholic Church engineers certain ecumenical movements now to bring unity and unification between religions. I believe this is false.

I do hope that Jesus' prayer in John 17, that the Christians would be one like Jesus and the Father are one. I know that Jesus was led by the Holy Spirit when he prayed that prayer. I do hold out hope that they can be and will be unity among the body of Christ one day.

There are many denominations and different doctrines and points of view in the Christian church.

We've discussed several things in these 50 Hot Potato Questions. I don't imagine everyone listening to these videos or reading this book would agree with my overall point of view on the 50 points raised. There's a multitude of Christians who believe all sorts of things, different points of view on different things and their difference in opinions and theologies keep them from being unified.

All Christians should be unified because Jesus Christ is our Savior. He died on a cross, and three days later, he was resurrected and ascended into heaven 40 days later and sits at the right-hand side of the Father and executes a judgment in the world. We should understand that Jesus is a high priest and listens to our prayers and adds to our prayers and intercedes to the Father for us. These are fundamental to the Christian faith that Jesus was born in a virgin birth and one day will rule the world, and the world will see him as the Messiah.

We can agree certain points are fundamental points of the Christian faith. We can agree and come together under those points and let our differing doctrines be put aside and come together in unity.

I'd Love to Hear from You

One of the ways that you can bless me as a writer is by writing an honest and candid review of my book on Amazon, where you purchased this book. I always read the reviews of my books, and I would love to hear what you have to say about this one.

Before I buy a book, I read the reviews first. You can make an informed decision about a book after reading enough honest reviews. One way to help me sell this book and give me positive feedback is by writing a review. It doesn't cost you a thing but helps the future readers of this book and me enormously.

To read my blog, request a life-coaching session, request your prophecy, or receive a personal message from your angel, you can also visit my website at http://personal-prophecy-today.com. All the funds raised through my ministry website will go toward the books I write and self-publish.

GET YOUR FREE BOOKS BY MATTHEW ROBERT PAYNE

To read more than 40 of Matthew Robert Payne's books for free, please visit https://matthewrobertpayne.com.

Matthew also has 86 books in total on Amazon Kindle for 99 cents. You can find them here https://tinyurl.com/p69rch5x

To write to me about this book or share any other thoughts, please contact me at my email address at survivors.sanctuary@gmail.com.

You can also friend request me on Facebook at Matthew Robert Payne[1]. Please send me a message if we have no friends, as many scammers now send me friend requests.

You can also do me a huge favor and share this book on Facebook as a recommended book to read. This will help other readers and me.

Please do not be afraid to contact me and connect with me. I enjoy speaking to my readers, and all my best friends have read most of my books over time. I can't contact you as I don't know who you are, but you can contact me ☺

---

1.   https://www.facebook.com/matthew.r.payne

How to Support Me

If this book has blessed you, can you ask the Lord whether you would like to support me financially? My income is found mostly from monthly sponsors on PayPal. I encourage you to consider sending me a once-off gift or being a monthly sponsor of my book-writing ministry.

I write to teach, encourage, and lift people. I write full-time and only write what the Holy Spirit puts on my heart. Most of my books are 99 cents, and of late, I have been making my books for free on Amazon. Therefore, my writing is a ministry, not a money-making venture. I would be greatly encouraged by your once-off support or your ongoing support. Please, take the time to commit this to prayer, and see if God would have you support me.

I would also be encouraged by your prayers that God would continue to inspire me and that He would also encourage people to support me. Pray for the readers of my books to be touched and for them to grow in intimacy with Jesus.

You can sow any amount to my ministry by sending me money via the PayPal link at this address: http://personal-prophecy-today.com/support-my-ministry[1].

About Matthew Robert Payne

Matthew Robert Payne, a teacher and prophet, enjoys writing what the Lord puts on his heart to share. He receives great pleasure from interacting with others on Facebook, hearing from people who have read his books, and prophesying over people's lives. He is a passionate lover of and disciple of Jesus Christ. He hopes that as you discover his books, you will intimately come to know Jesus, the Father, and Matthew through his transparent writing style.

Matthew grew up in a traditional Baptist church and gave his heart to Jesus Christ at eight. But he left home at eighteen, living a wild life for many years and engaging in bad habits and addictions. At twenty-seven, he was baptized in water and, at the same time, baptized in the Holy Spirit. Matthew learned about the five-fold ministry offices and received a revelation of their value today.

He started his journey as a prophet twenty years ago, learning about this gift and putting it into practice. He can confidently prophesy to friends and strangers with thousands of prophecies. He has been writing for several years and self-published his first book in 2011. Today he spends his time earning money to self-publish and writes a new book approximately every month. He also produces many videos that you can view on YouTube.

You can connect with him on Facebook. You can sow into his book-writing ministry, read his blog, receive a message from your angel, or even receive your own nine-minute personal prophecy from Matthew at http://personal-prophecy-today.com.

Acknowledgments

I want to thank Jesus, the Holy Spirit, the Father, and my scribe, angel Bethany, for this book's knowledge and wisdom. I want to thank all those above for the finances and the people who support me in ministry.

I want to thank my friends Roy, Deb, Shayne, Dundy, Lisa, and others who support me with their love. Your love is priceless to me, a broken man.

Thanks also to my readers who inspire me to write.

Don't miss out!

Visit the website below and you can sign up to receive emails whenever Matthew Robert Payne publishes a new book. There's no charge and no obligation.

https://books2read.com/r/B-A-TLBC-JSVCC

BOOKS 2 READ

Connecting independent readers to independent writers.

About the Publisher

Accepting manuscripts in the most categories. We love to help people get their words available to the world.

Revival Waves of Glory focus is to provide more options to be published. We do traditional paperbacks, hardcovers, audio books and ebooks all over the world. A traditional royalty-based publisher that offers self-publishing options, Revival Waves provides a very author friendly and transparent publishing process, with President Bill Vincent involved in the full process of your book. Send us your manuscript and we will contact you as soon as possible.

Contact: Bill Vincent at rwgpublishing@yahoo.com